Love & War

PARTICIPANT'S GUIDE

JOHN & STASI
ELDREDGE

ZONDERVAN® RANSOMED HEART
LOVE GOD. LIVE FREE.

WWW.RANSOMEDHEART.COM

ZONDERVAN.com/
AUTHORTRACKER
follow your favorite authors

ZONDERVAN

Love & War Participant's Guide
Copyright © 2010 by John and Stasi Eldredge

Requests for information should be addressed to:
Zondervan, *Grand Rapids, Michigan 49530*

ISBN 978-0-310-32921-3

Published in association with Yates & Yates, www.yates2.com.

Cover design: W. G. Cookman
Interior design: Eastco Multimedia Solutions

Printed in the United States of America

10 11 12 13 14 15 16 17 • 20 19 18 17 16 15 14 13 12 11 10 9 8 7 6 5 4 3

CONTENTS

INTRODUCTION

Stasi and I love exploring new places together.

We love to travel; we love to canoe; and we also love to find a great new movie or taco stand! Exploring together opens up a spaciousness in our relationship. It gets us out of the mundane, the daily grind. It awakens desire, and it almost always opens up opportunities for great conversation. There's a hopefulness in our hearts as we set out, an expectation: "This is going to be good!"

With that spirit of hopeful anticipation we offer you this participant's guide to the *Love and War* video study.

It works like this: the guide you are holding dovetails with the book *Love and War*, and with the eight sessions you'll be watching in the video study. (You'll want to have a copy of the book and a copy of the video. If you are leading a group, we have provided a leader's guide in the video case.)

Now, we know folks are busy, so we've tried to keep this simple and straightforward. Doable. Each session in this guide has three parts:

PERSONAL PREPARATION

Before your group meets (we're assuming you are doing this in a group—even if that "group" is just you and your spouse) you'll want to read the corresponding chapter in the book and answer a few questions in this guide.

GROUP TIME

Watch the session video together. Then talk about it. We've suggested a few questions to help guide your group's conversation time. (Again, if you are a leader, there's more guidance for you in the leader's guide.)

AFTERWARD

Some of the best conversations take place *after* group—as you are driving home, or later in the week. "Honey, what did you mean when you said ... ?"

You also know that some of the biggest blowups can happen afterward, too. So, we provide guidance to help steer you and your spouse away from the potential hazards and guide you toward something truly helpful. Your "Personal Preparation" should take place alone; your "Group Time" allows for some good conversation; but the best time may be "Afterward," as the two of you talk about things together.

We also suggest some fun activities for the two of you to try afterward as well.

A LITTLE LOVING COUNSEL

We believe the book *Love and War*, the video, and this guide will provide rich opportunities for reflection and conversation that will open up the possibility for all sorts of wonderful things to happen in your marriage.

Now yes, it can be a little awkward at times, like shifting your weight around in a canoe; it can feel a little uncertain. And yes, you must remember that you have an enemy (we'll get to that session soon) and he loves to twist and steal and thwart marital happiness. So don't be surprised when things feel a little scary at times, or don't go the way you hoped they would. God is for you. As we say in the book:

> We all know that loving is hard. Marriage is hard. It is op-
> posed. The devil hates marriage; he hates the beautiful picture of
> Jesus and his Bride that it represents. He hates love and life and
> beauty in all its forms. The world hates marriage. It hates unity
> and faithfulness and monogamy. Our flesh is not our ally here

either—it rebels when we put others before ourselves. Our flesh hates dying.

But God loves marriage! The Holy Trinity is for it. God loves intimacy and friendship and unity and self-sacrifice and laughter and pleasure and joy and the picture of the Sacred Romance that you have the opportunity to present to the watching world. God is with you. He is for you! (from *Love and War*)

God is with you! He is for you! So we encourage you to pray for your marriage as you do this study. Pray that God will come, speak, unite and heal your marriage!

Lord Jesus, come. Come and lead us as we do this study. Give us both an open heart and mind; give us the grace to go where you are leading. Give us courage to face what needs to be faced, and give us hope for all that you have for us. We pray you would thwart the plans of the enemy, every week, and help us navigate past the hazards and into some really good conversations. Come, Holy Spirit, and prepare us for all the redemption and goodness you have for us in this experience. Give us new eyes for our marriage. Lead us. In Jesus' name we pray.

This is going to be good!

SESSION

1

HOPE AND VISION

What would it look like for the two of you to find *your* way to something beautiful?

Don't start with, *How can that happen? How* will come in time; we can help you with how. You have to begin with *desire.* Start with what is written on your heart. What was it that you once dreamed of as a young man or woman? What was it you wanted when you fell in love?

PERSONAL PREPARATION

Love and War is a twelve-chapter book. This guide and the video have eight sessions. So, in a few cases, we've combined chapters from the book to fit this study. This week, read chapters one and two in *Love and War,* and answer the following questions before your group time.

❖ It is always good to start with a first reaction. Was there something that touched a chord, brought an "aha" moment, something that stood out in particular? (Often this is the very thing the Lord is using to speak to us.) What struck you in chapters one and two?

Maybe we ought to just start this book here: Marriage is fabulously hard.

Everybody who's been married knows this. Though years into marriage it still catches us off guard, all of us. And newly married couples, when they discover how hard it is, they seem genuinely surprised. Shocked, and disheartened by the fact. *Are we doing something wrong? Did I marry the right person?* The sirens that lure us into marriage—romance, love, passion, sex, longing, companionship—they seem so far from the actual reality of married life we fear we've made a colossal mistake, caught the wrong bus, missed our flight. And so the hardness also comes as something of an embarrassment (don't you feel embarrassed to admit how hard your marriage is?). *Maybe it's just us.*

❖ Has this been true for you—has your marriage felt hard at times? And did that shock you, surprise you, dishearten you? What has been your reaction to the awkwardness of marriage?

❖ We said in the book that when marriage gets hard we often feel as though we'd made a mistake, or that we are blowing it. Has that been part of your experience?

All those fairy tales about a boy and girl who find themselves thrown together into an adventure in a dangerous land, and how they must come to work together if they have any hope of making it through, but they are both carrying a tragic flaw, an Achilles heel that pricks the other constantly and they barely *do* make it through—those fairy tales pretty much have it right.

In fact, if you look back at the first marriage, that almost fairy-tale-like story in Genesis, you'll see that Adam and Eve had a pretty rough go at it. And they didn't even have parents to screw them up as children or friends giving them ridiculous advice. My goodness, the Fall of man seems to come during the honeymoon, or shortly thereafter. (And how many honeymoon stories reenact that little drama?) They hit rough water as soon as they set sail, poor things. If this is the story of the first marriage, it's a bit sobering.

But it also gives us some encouragement, too. It's normal for marriage to be hard. Even the best of marriages.

❖ What does this truth do for you?

Because marriage is hard, sometimes painfully hard, your first great battle is not to lose heart. That begins with recovering desire—the desire for the love that is written on your heart. Let desire return. Let it remind you of all that you wanted, all that you were created for. And then consider this—what if God could bring you your heart's desire? What if the two of you could find your way to something beautiful?

Stasi and I have become best friends. We started out that way, long ago, before we married, but we lost it somewhere along the road. More than once. God has helped us find it again. We have a shared life now. We are on the same page, living for the same things. We have found our way to something beautiful. We have found that the promise of the Gospel is true.

What would it look like for the two of you to find *your* way to something beautiful?

Don't start with, *How can that happen?* How will come in time; we can help you with how. You have to begin with *desire.* Start with what is written on your heart. What was it that you once dreamed of as a young man or woman? What was it you wanted when you fell in love?

❖ Well? Write down your desires and dreams for your marriage. Some of them might come from movies, as we talked about toward the end of chapter one. Some might come from desires you had when you first got married. Some might be desires that you have matured into over the years. What is it that you long for in marriage?

❖ Is there a scene or two from a movie that captures what you want for your marriage? What is it? What about the scene grabs you?

> The Bible begins with a marriage, and ends with a marriage. We never noticed that before.
>
> Here is the story God is telling, the story that will explain our lives, the story in which all other stories find their meaning. Open the book to chapter one, page one, and suddenly—there is a marriage.
>
> Now flip to the end of the story. The epic tale reaches its climax with the end of the world as we know it. After the white horse and its Rider appear, after the legendary battle of Armageddon, as the whole creation reaches its dénouement, suddenly we find—a marriage.
>
> And so we see from start to finish, the part of this great story we have been given to play begins and ends with a marriage.

❖ Had you noticed that before? Have you seen marriage playing a crucial role in the story God is telling?

❖ In chapter two we describe this world (and the Christian faith) as a love story set in the midst of war. Is that how you've understood it?

In all of the great stories the boy and girl are thrown together in a great adventure they did not choose, and they desperately need each other if they are going to make it through. Shasta and Aravis are driven together by the lion; Mossy and Tangle, sent on a quest with the Golden Key; Hansel and Gretel, holding hands for fear, making their way through the dark woods; Beauty and the Beast, learning to love so that they both might be free; why, even Jack and Jill need each other to get that pail of water. We love those tales; they are loved all over the world. But most of you haven't yet made the connection—the reason your heart leaps to these stories is because they are telling you about *your* story.

Really.

Your marriage is part of a larger story, too, a story as romantic as any that's ever stirred your heart, and at least as dangerous. The sooner you come to terms with this, the sooner you can understand what is happening in your marriage.

❖ How would this change the way you look at your marriage? And the way you interpret what is currently happening *in* your marriage?

THE CORE IDEAS

This session corresponds to chapters one and two of *Love and War*. Now, we hate to try and "boil it down" to a few key points (we wrote a whole book, after all), but here are the core ideas for this week:

—∞∞∞—

- Marriage is fabulously hard. For everyone. Don't let this throw you.

- The Gospel is an offer of hope. God cares passionately about your marriage!

- To find your way to something beautiful, it helps to begin with desire. What is it you long for in marriage?

- We live in a love story, set in a world at war.

- Your marriage plays a crucial role in that Larger Story.

GROUP TIME

Watch the session one video together. If you would like, use the following space to take a few notes on anything that stood out to you.

After watching the video, discuss as a group any or all of the following questions:

1. Let's start with a first reaction. What spoke to you in this week's chapters, or this video session?

2. The group talked about how surprised they were that marriage is hard. That it was a lot easier to date than to be married. Have you found that to be true? In what ways?

3. Is that easy to admit? Is there shame connected to that? And does it help to hear that even really good marriages can be really hard?

4. Lori and Stasi both shared that one of the big surprises coming into marriage was that they thought they knew the man they married, and thought they knew themselves, but discovered they had a lot to learn. Can you relate to that?

5. The group talked about fighting for marriage—Morgan said how he has come to realize that the good times have to be fought for, even something as simple as a date or a night out together. Has that been true for you?

6. Chapter two of the book laid out a vision for marriage, that it is a love story set in a world at war. How does that help you understand your marriage?

7. Maybe the biggest idea from this session is that desire is crucial for marriage. Because marriage is hard, because we have to fight for it, the recovery of desire is really essential. The group shared a bit about their desires and dreams for marriage; was there a desire shared in the group that you resonated with? Why?

8. What are your desires and dreams for your marriage? Is there a memory, or a scene from a movie that helps to picture that desire? (It would be good if everyone in the group could answer this question).

In closing, pray together! Maybe a couple of you could pray, and invite God to fill your group, lead your journey together, and that God would fill you with dreams and desires for your marriage.

AFTERWARD

❖ What would you like to talk to your spouse about?

WARNING: Timing is *everything* in marriage. I can't begin to name the number of times I wanted to talk to Stasi about something, and simply brought it up because I was passionate about it … BUT I didn't stop to ask Jesus if the timing was right. And when the timing was wrong, it did *not* go well! So, you'll want to practice this one crucial act of following Christ as you move through *Love and War—ask Jesus* when to bring things up! Ask him *how* to bring things up!

If you feel you want to bring up something big, a real whopper, you will want to wait until there is time to talk about it. Maybe go out to dinner this week? Ask your spouse to have coffee? But we don't recommend starting with "big whoppers." This study is just getting started, after all. It's only session one! Let us suggest a couple of things that might help the two of you really enjoy and deepen your experience of the truths of this session:

"Honey, what struck you tonight?" "Did the Lord say something to you?" "Which couple did you most connect with in the video?"

Talk about the desires for your marriage that you shared during group (if you did share them during group; if you didn't share them, talk about them now!) Are there other desires you have which you didn't have time to share? Talk about these with your spouse. Not with the sense of "you are not living up to this" or "this is what I demand of you" but simply in the vulnerable and humble spirit of "this is what I would love to see happen in our marriage."

ACTIVITY:

Watch a movie together. Make it a date. One of you could suggest a film because it portrays something that you'd love to experience in your marriage. Or, maybe each of you share a scene from a movie that captures something of your heart's desire for your marriage.

Look at your wedding pictures together. And your honeymoon pictures! Just enjoy them, remember.

This week, you'll want to do the "Personal Preparation" part for session two.

NOTES

NOTES

SESSION

A Perfect Storm

Our mutual brokenness plays off of each other so perfectly it's frightening. It's like throwing a dog and a cat in a dryer. Is he absolutely mad? Why would God do such a thing?

Because marriage is a divine conspiracy.

It is a conspiracy divinely arranged and with divine intent.

God lures us into marriage through love and sex and loneliness, or simply the fact that someone finally paid attention—all those reasons that you got married in the first place. It doesn't really matter, he'll do whatever it takes. He lures us into marriage and then he uses it to *transform us.*

PERSONAL PREPARATION

This week, read chapter three in *Love and War,* and answer the following questions.

❖ It is always good to start with a first reaction. Often there is something that touched a chord, brought an "aha moment," something that stood out in particular. (Often this is the very thing the Lord is using to speak to us.) What struck you in chapter three?

Stasi likes to talk. I'll be standing in the kitchen in the morning, and she'll start a conversation from the bedroom and she'll just carry right on even though I am running the blender and no rabbit could possibly hear a thing she's saying. Then she'll walk into the room and ask, "Well?" And then there are the lights. Whatever room we are in, Stasi likes the lights dim. I, on the other hand, love a room as bright as can be. Now, we'll be sitting in the room together and Stasi will just get up and dim down the lights. Drives me absolutely nuts.

John likes to smell things before he eats them. Like a cat. He'll open a box of cereal and smell it before he takes a bite. I'll offer him to share my bag of chips and he'll smell them before taking one. It drives me crazy. And he has this habit of getting up and walking out of the room without saying where he's going or why. We will be in the middle of a family time together, and he'll just up and walk out.

Now, add to our personality differences the fact that he's a *man* and I'm a *woman* and you get two people so opposite from one another they are often a complete mystery to the other.

I enjoy watching cake decorating shows. John is hooked on *Man vs. Wild.* He likes the occasional cigar. I don't like the smell. I love scented candles. John abhors them. A treat for me is getting a pedicure and an amazing day for John is going bow hunting.

And we live together. In the same house. It's a wonder we don't kill each other. Sometimes we drive each other crazy simply by being ourselves.

❖ Can you relate? What are the things you do that drive each other crazy?

For some reason, I [John] remember the conversation vividly. We were driving up Interstate 25 through Colorado Springs, a young friend and I, when he made the following pronouncement: "I'm so glad that Julie's not broken." He was talking about the girl he was about to get engaged to. I tried to suppress the raising of my eyebrows, said nothing, in hopes he would continue with his train of thought. "I mean, think of all the gals in our community—most of them are really a mess. Julie is not. She's good." I just kept looking forward, nodded, said something like, "That's great." He wasn't ready for what I had to say. I mean, enjoy the balloon while you can; I don't need to be the one to pop it. Inside, something sad sort of sighed. *Brother, you are in for one heck of a shock.*

It is six years later, and he would describe this past year as the most difficult of his entire life. Turns out there was a lot more brokenness there than he thought.

There always is.

The first big shock we receive in marriage is that it's hard. The second great shock usually follows hard on the heels of the first—that we are, both of us, a royal mess. Why is he so defensive? Why doesn't she enjoy sex? How come he withers under criticism? Why is she so clingy? What is this simmering rage just under the surface? Where did this addiction come from? Why won't you talk to me? Who *are* you?!

❖ Have you encountered this "second big shock" of marriage—that you are, both of you, a royal mess? How did the shock come—and how did it make you feel?

A woman with deep wounds of disappointment marries a man she cannot possibly please; her fear that she will never really be loved meets his commitment to never need anyone. That's like someone with a fear of heights taking a job cleaning windows on the Empire State Building. A man with deep abandonment wounds from his father's addiction marries a woman whose deep addiction will cause her to withdraw from him. His fear that what he has to offer will never be enough meets the chasm in her heart that no amount of love can fill. The way these things play into each other is chilling. You could not script a more frightening scenario.

Opposites attract all right—our mutual brokenness is drawn together like a match and gunpowder.

❖ Can you name some of the ways your brokenness collides with your spouse's brokenness?

When it comes to high-level expeditions, one piece of advice that veterans unanimously urge is this: "Choose your tent mate carefully." For you are going to spend weeks to months on end shut-in by foul weather in the forced intimacy of a tiny fabric cocoon with this person. By the time it's over everything about them will drive you mad—the way they eat, the way they breathe, the way they hum show tunes or pick their nails. To keep yourselves from a Donner Party ending, you must start with people you are utterly compatible with.

God does the opposite—he puts us with our opposite. Our mutual brokenness plays off of each other so perfectly it's frightening. It's like throwing a dog and a cat in a dryer. Is he absolutely mad? Why would God do such a thing?

Because marriage is a divine conspiracy.

It is a conspiracy divinely arranged and with divine intent.

God lures us into marriage through love and sex and loneliness, or simply the fact that someone finally paid attention—all those reasons that you got married in the first place. It doesn't really matter, he'll do whatever it takes. He lures us into marriage and then he uses it to *transform us*.

❖ Is that the way you've looked at your marriage—as God's conspiracy to transform you? What does this revelation do to your perspective of things?

We all have a style of relating; we have a way that we do life. Our carefully crafted approach colors the way we work, the way we love, the way we relate, the way we handle stress, the way we look at life, and the way we simply have a conversation with people. Our style of relating is born out of brokenness and sin, and it is *the number one thing* that gets in the way of real love and companionship, the shared adventure and all the beauty of marriage. It's really this simple—the number one thing that gets in the way is your way. I don't mean insisting on getting your way—that the lights be dim or finding a better parking spot. I mean your way of going about life, your style of relating.

We are, all of us, utterly committed and deeply devoted to our "style," our "way," our approach to life. We have absolutely no intention of giving it up.

Not even to love. So God creates an environment where we have to. It's called marriage.

❖   Is that a new thought to you—that you have a "style of relating"? Can you name what yours is?

And what does learning to love look like? Well, for one thing, it looks like compassion for your spouse's brokenness while choosing to turn from your own self-protective style of relating.

We must come to face our style, of course. As men, we look to where we are passive, and where we are domineering or harsh or violent. As women, we face where we are controlling, and where we are desperately clingy. And as God reveals these things, we make those thousand little choices to turn from our style of relating. We make deliberate choices to love. If you avoid conflict either as a passive man or a controlling woman, then you say, "Conflict is okay. Let's talk about these things. I'll go there with you." If you have been avoiding intimacy, then you say, "I need you. I don't want to be this island, this impenetrable fortress. I choose to engage." If it's controlling, I let go of control. If it's hiding, I come out of hiding. If it's anger, I set my anger aside and I choose to be vulnerable.

Now, it would be very, very helpful for you both to know the story of each other's lives. Ladies, do you know the story of your husband's life? Gents, do you know your wife's?

❖ Do you? How does knowing their story help give you compassion and understanding for your spouse's style of relating?

There are two kinds of people in this world—the clueless and the repentant. Those who are open to looking at their life and those who are not. Folks who know they need God to change them, and folks who are expecting everyone else to change. We have great hope for the first group; the second bunch is *choosing* ignorance; the damage they are doing is almost unforgiveable.

This is why the "apply some principles" approach to marriage improvement doesn't work. As long as we choose to turn a blind eye to how we are fallen as a man or woman, and the unique style of relating we have forged out of our sin and brokenness, we will continue to do damage to our marriages. And add to our spouse's hopelessness that things will never change. You don't want to add cynicism and resignation to your marriage. You want your spouse to experience, *She is really changing! He is really thinking about his impact on me!* That inspires so much hope. It awakens so much desire. Something begins to stir in our hearts, *Wow, this could get good. I mean, we could really go places here!*

This happens when we make the shift from changing you to changing me.

❖   Be honest now—how much of your frustration, anger, disappoint-ment comes from wanting your spouse to change? How much of your energy is spent trying to *get* your spouse to change versus accepting the change God is seeking in you?

THE CORE IDEAS

This session corresponds to chapter three in *Love and War*. The essential ideas in this chapter are:

—∞—

- The second great shock of marriage is that we are—both of us—a royal mess.

- We all have a style of relating, a way that we do life. Our style of relating is borne out of brokenness and sin, and it is *the number one thing* that gets in the way of real love and companionship, the shared adventure and all the beauty of marriage.

- Marriage is a divine conspiracy, arranged by God for your transformation.

- Happiness in marriage waits upon the shift from changing you to changing me.

GROUP TIME

Watch the session two video together. If you would like, use the following space to take notes on anything that stood out to you.

After watching the video, discuss as a group any or all of the following questions:

1. Let's start with a first reaction. What spoke to you in this week's chapter, or this video session?

2. Did you find yourself connecting with one couple's story in particular? Why?

3. The couples on the video talked about the ways they are opposite. They had a lightheartedness about their differences; they seemed able to laugh at them. What are some of the ways you and your spouse are opposites?

4. The chapter calls marriage a "perfect storm." God has actually arranged for the two of you to be together with all your differences. It is his conspiracy. Was that a new thought to you?

5. Craig admitted that his cleaning out the refrigerator and "organizing" Lori's life was a subtle way of getting her to change, telling her to get her act together. Is the tension in your relationships due to the fact that you are trying to somehow change the other person?

6. The couples in the small group are all aware that they have a style of relating, and they are also aware of how it is affecting their spouse. Are you aware of your "style," and how it is affecting your spouse?

7. Morgan said that God sent Cherie to save him from himself; that one of the core reasons for their deep differences is that God is using them to surface things in Morgan he needs to change. What would happen in your marriage if that becomes the way you see your spouse?

AFTERWARD

❖ What would you like to talk to your spouse about?

WARNING: Talking about our differences, and the ways we drive each other crazy is important for a marriage. We don't want small irritations to build and build and become volcanoes. BUT be careful how you talk about this; you want to bring it up *not* with an accusing tone, but more with a loving lightheartedness.

The best person to help us identify our style of relating is our spouse. Ask each other, "Honey, what would you say my style is?"

ACTIVITY:

In this session we talked about how very, very helpful it is for both of you to know the story of each other's lives. For us, we took an evening each—several hours—and told each other the story of our lives. Starting with our childhood, we spoke of memorable moments—the painful ones as well as the happy ones. Pieces of the puzzle of each other's personalities began to fit into place. "Oh, that's why you hate to talk on the phone" or "So, is that why you feel so defensive toward me?" Now I get it.

Understanding our spouse by understanding the unfolding story of their life is priceless. We can come alongside them and help them to overcome difficulties so much easier and more tenderly when we understand "where they are coming from." When we begin to understand one another's brokenness we'll find a great deal more compassion for what was previously simply driving us nuts.

Set aside some time—an evening for each of you—to tell each other the story of your lives.

This week, you'll want to do the "Personal Preparation" part for session three.

NOTES

NOTES

SESSION

THE GREATEST GIFT YOU CAN GIVE

There are all sorts of joy to be found in your marriage, once you stop looking to your spouse to make you happy.

PERSONAL PREPARATION

This week, read chapter four in *Love and War*, and answer the following questions.

❖ It is always good to start with a first reaction. What struck you in chapter four?

❖ What was your response to my confession that I hate Valentine's Day? Are there occasions you've come to resent—birthdays, vacations, ministry events, business dinners, having sex—because of the pressure you feel?

I don't think most of us have any idea how much pressure we are bringing to our marriages.

There's the pressure one of you feels from the other to "be happy."

There's the pressure to like your family. Or your friends.

Christian couples feel the added pressure to have a model marriage.

There's the pressure a woman puts on a man to climb the ladder.

The pressure a man puts on a woman to be beautiful.

Or how about the pressure to "share everything."

We talked about the pressure to make Christmas magical, recreate some summer vacation memory by revisiting that very place every year.

There's the pressure—and how bizarre is this, really—that someone love you.

And then there's the Biggest Pressure of All—the pressure we feel to make each other happy.

❖ Which of these pressures can you relate to? Can you name a few of your own that aren't on our list?

❖ What is the *effect* of this pressure on you? And what is the effect of this pressure on your marriage?

The human heart has an infinite capacity for happiness and an unending need for love, because it is created for an infinite God who is unending love. The desperate turn is when we bring the aching abyss of our hearts to one another with the hope, the plea, "Make me happy. Fill this ache." And often out of love we *do* try to make one another happy, and then we wonder why it never lasts.

It can't be done.

You will kill yourself trying.

We are broken people, with a famished craving in our hearts.

Every woman now has an insatiable need for relationship, one that can never be filled. It is an ache in her soul designed to drive her to God. Men instinctively know the bottomless well is there, and pull back. *I don't want to be engulfed by that. Besides, no matter how much I offer, it'll never be enough.* This is Eve's sorrow. This is the break in her cup. She aches for intimacy, to be known and loved and *chosen*. And it also explains her deepest fear—abandonment.

Men face a different sort of emptiness. We are forever frustrated in our ability to conquer life. That's the "sweat of your brow ... thorns and thistles" thing. "Cursed is the ground because of you; through painful toil you will eat of it all the days of your life. It will produce thorns and thistles for you" (Genesis 3:17–18). A man aches for affirmation, for validation, to know that he has come through. This also explains his deepest fear—failure.

❖ Are you aware of the famished craving in your heart? Can you relate to the ways we've described a woman's hunger, or a man's?

Of course you are disappointed with your marriage.

It's not a sin to admit that. It's not a betrayal. And it need not be an earthquake. (In fact, if you cannot admit the disappointment of your marriage, you have made an idol of it. It has become "The Thing we cannot question.") Of course you are disappointed; your spouse is disappointed, too. How can we possibly be enough for one another? Two broken cups cannot possibly fill one another. Happiness flows through us like water through a sieve.

❖ Have you been able to admit—at least to yourself—the disappointment you feel in your marriage?

"I keep telling him he's doing great. It doesn't seem to sink in." "I don't know how many times I've shown her I am here for her. It's like she doesn't believe me or something." It's so disheartening. We feel responsible for our spouse's unhappiness. *I'm not doing enough. I'm not enough. If I were a better man, a better woman, she or he'd be happy. It must be me.* Let this go on for a while and we move from guilt to resentment. *Can't you be happy with anything? It's never enough for you, is it?* How you are doing becomes the report card on me. If you are not happy, I must not be doing it right, doing enough.

It is a vicious cycle, actually worse for those who are trying hard to love.

The good news is, of course you're not enough. You never, ever will be. Of course you can't make each other happy. This should come as a tremendous relief, actually. *Oh, I thought it was just us. That somehow we'd missed the class on marital happiness and now we're flunking the whole course.* Nope, it's not just you. It's everyone. Knowing this allows you to take the report card away from your spouse. How they are doing is not the verdict on you.

Let that sink in for a moment—how they are doing is not the report card on you.

Their unhappiness doesn't mean you're an "F" as a person, as a spouse.

❖   Let that sink in. What does this truth do for you? Do you realize how your spouse's happiness has felt like the verdict on you?

❖   And, knowing that they are not the report card on you—how does that make you feel? What does it free you of?

What we are saying is simply this: You have to have some place you can turn. For comfort. Understanding. For the healing of your brokenness. For love. To offer life, you must have life. And you can only get this from God. "My soul finds rest in God alone." Trying to sort your way through marriage without God in your life is like trying to be gracious when you are utterly sleep-deprived. At some point, you lose your ability to be kind; you lose all perspective. As David Wilcox sings,

>*We cannot trade empty for empty*
>*We must come to the waterfall*
>*For there's a break in the cup that holds love ... inside us all*

And so the greatest gift you can give to your marriage is to have a real relationship with Jesus Christ.

This is the kindest thing you could ever do for your spouse.

❖   Why is this the kindest thing you can do for your spouse—and they for you? And when you *don't* turn to God—where do you turn? What is the effect on your marriage?

❖ What simple step can you take to deepen your relationship with God? What can you do to begin to turn to him more often as your source of life? Is it taking walks? A regular time of prayer? What is it for you that helps you find life in God?

THE CORE IDEAS

- Pressure kills everything it touches. Most of us are unaware of the amount of pressure we are putting on our marriage.

- The human heart has an infinite capacity for love and happiness, because we are made for God.

- Of course you are disappointed in your marriage. Your spouse is disappointed, too. Two broken cups cannot possibly fill one another.

- You have to have some place you can turn. For comfort. Understanding. For the healing of your brokenness. For love. To offer life, you must have life. And you can only get this from God.

- The greatest gift you can give your marriage is to have a real relationship with Jesus Christ.

GROUP TIME

Watch the session three video together. If you would like, use the following space to take notes on anything that stood out to you.

After watching the video, discuss as a group any or all of the following questions:

1. Let's start with a first reaction. What spoke to you in this week's chapter, or this video session?

2. Did you find yourself connecting with one couple's story in particular?

3. Morgan described the pressure he feels when he believes that Cherie's happiness is his responsibility. Can you relate to feeling that—your spouse's happiness is your responsibility?

4. And so what happens when they are unhappy—what does that mean about you?

5. What does pressure do to the romance of your marriage?

6. Where are you feeling the pressure these days?

7. The Big Idea of this chapter is that we are all leaky cups, and only God can possibly fill us. Does this help you understand the disappointments and tensions in your marriage?

8. Craig talked about the hope he began to experience when he realized that much of what he was longing for could be found in God. He

said the effect has been that things which were once mountains in their marriage began to shrink back into molehills. Cherie said it's changed the way she relates to Morgan; how when Morgan is in a bad mood, she doesn't take it personally. Have you experienced the hope of this? What was the effect on your marriage?

9. Cherie said that she and Morgan can now "cheer each other on," become their biggest advocates in pursuing God. How can you cheer your spouse on in their relationship with God?

AFTERWARD

❖ What would you like to talk to your spouse about?

WARNING: Talking about the disappointments you experience in your marriage can only be done in love; otherwise, it feels accusing. You'll want to walk gently here. The spirit of this is, "Honey, I'm realizing that I've been looking to you for things that only God can provide."

We're hoping that as you progress through this study, you are able to move into deeper waters with one another. A really good conversation to have with your spouse would be, "Sweetheart, where do you feel pressure in our marriage?"

Another good question would be, "How can I help to cheer you on in your pursuit of God?"

ACTIVITY:

What is it that helps bring you back to the presence of God? Is it worship music? A good book? Time spent outdoors? In the Scriptures? This week's activity—appropriately—is not for you as a couple, but for you as individuals. Get some time with God!

And then, yes, talk about it. Share your spiritual journey with each other. What did you do? How did you experience God?

This week, you'll want to do the "Personal Preparation" part for session four.

NOTES

NOTES

SESSION

4

Sharing an Adventure

So—what's the mission of your marriage? What are the two of you called to, *together*? Can you name it? "We're in this together," is essential for the boy and girl in the fairy tale. Finding a shared mission as a couple is essential to a vibrant marriage. It might be the very thing to rescue a floundering couple, and it will surely take you both to a whole new level of companionship regardless of where you are.

Our hearts are made for adventure. Surviving the week so you can hit the food court at the mall on the weekend is not enough.

PERSONAL PREPARATION

Read chapters five and seven in *Love and War*, and answer the following questions.

❖ Start with a first reaction. What struck you in chapters five and seven?

John and I have walked through some very hard times together—the death of dear friends; the loss of long-term relationships; many hospital visits; moving cross-country three times. We've also shared some really wonderful times—traveling in Scotland and Ireland, speaking together at conferences, snorkeling in Mexico, realizing a lifelong dream of buying a ranch. And then there are all the "in-between times"—making the boys' lunches in the evening, texting each other when we're out and about, saying our bedtime prayers together for twenty-five years.

❖ Chapter five is about *companionship*. Jot down some of the things you and your spouse have been through together—both the hard times and the good times.

Companionship is far more the actual brick and mortar of two lives lived together. Companionship is the glue that allows a marriage to make it—not just through the hard times, but make it in the sense of finding your way to something rich together.

❖ Would you say you and your spouse are companions? On a scale of 1–10, how much would you say you experience companionship in your marriage?

There are always "reasons" behind the choices that cause us to end up living in different worlds. The details may vary, but the story is fairly common. Despite our vows, our hopes and dreams, most couples end up living separate lives.

What typically happens is that both the man and woman get busy. You go to work; you come home exhausted. If you have children, they get what's left of you before bedtime. If you're successful in work or ministry, it eats you alive. If you're barely surviving, it devours your hope and energy along with your time. Then we all look for a little something to refill our cups, doing what we enjoy or just vegging in front of the tube. And our spouse gets the dregs. We end up feeling like "two separate careerists in the same bed," as Wendell Berry described it.

❖   What has gotten in the way of developing companionship with your spouse?

Over the years we've found other ways to build companionship. We love to travel. We love going out for Chinese food. We share with each other movies that we like, or something from a book that has stirred us. John loves the wilderness; we found a way to enjoy it together using lodges. In this way we can spend a day out on the trail, but at night I get a shower and a bed!

❖ What are some ways you and your spouse could begin to build companionship into your marriage? What can you do, together? Is there something you'd like to invite your spouse into—taking walks, taking a trip, dinner out once a month, taking lessons together?

If you have been married for more than a year or two, you've probably fallen into a routine by now. She gets up at six; he gets up at six forty-five. She starts the coffee; he typically skips breakfast. Tuesday night you watch "your show"; Wednesday night you pay the bills; Friday night you rent a movie; Saturday you do chores; Sunday night you call your folks. You go to bed at the same time every night. You use the same shampoo you've used for years, the same toothpaste. You eat the same kind of bread, the same brand of spaghetti sauce. You get your socks from the same drawer you've been getting them from for thirty years. You drink your coffee the same way you always have. You make love the same way. And then you end up surprised by the agitation and irritation of cabin fever in your marriage. Boredom is the death knell for a couple. It is certainly the precursor to an affair, or an addiction. This little piggy went to market, this little piggy stayed home, this little piggy ate roast beef, and this little piggy went postal because this is exactly what the piggies have always done every day for the last forty-seven years.

❖ Well—can you relate? Has your marriage fallen into routine?

We still have all the joys of learning to sail the seas and write novels and discover quantum physics. But now we've also been called up into the more urgent mission of the invasion. Jesus has handed us the playbook; he has commissioned us to carry on in his stead. Every one of us. Which is to say that our mission now is far more grave than it was when Eden was our home, and of far greater consequence. Isn't this at the heart of every fairy tale? The boy and girl find themselves thrown into an adventure and frankly way over their heads. The two of you are part of something beautiful and dangerous.

This is crucial to a Christian understanding of marriage.

This is a difficult mindset to dislodge, this idea that the goal of marriage is a happy little home. Just look at the number of home improvement shows, the *size* of the many home improvement stores, the endless parade of make-your-home-dreamy catalogs. Most couples spend the best days of their lives trying to make their home a nicer place. It's not that this is bad; but the Christian couple has to reconcile it with Jesus' teaching on the kingdom: "But seek first his kingdom and his righteousness, and all these things will be given to you as well" (Matthew 6:34).

❖ Have you thought about marriage in this way—that your marriage was meant to have a *mission*? If so, what would you say that mission is? How much of your actual time, energy, and money is spent making a "happy little home"?

"We're in this together" is one of the strongest cords that binds two hearts together. This is as true for the man and woman who know they have a great task to accomplish as it is for two climbers roped together on the razor's edge of some Himalayan ridge, or two soldiers in a foxhole. To share a passion, a concern, a cause binds two hearts together quite unlike anything else. "We're in this together" lifts your marriage to a higher level than merely playing house.

❖ What would you say you and your spouse are "in this together" about, or over?

So—what's the mission of your marriage? What are the two of you called to, *together*? Can you name it? "We're in this together," is essential for the boy and girl in the fairy tale. Finding a shared mission as a couple is essential to a vibrant marriage. It might be the very thing to rescue a floundering couple, and it will surely take you both to a whole new level of companionship regardless of where you are.

Our hearts are made for adventure. Surviving the week so you can hit the food court at the mall on the weekend is not enough.

❖ Can you name the mission of your marriage? Can you begin to say what you would love for it *to* be?

Step two in finding a shared adventure is to cultivate an adventurous marriage. So—adventure together. Do a little dreaming, like we do around New Year's. Where would you love to travel? What about taking up dancing, or an instrument, learning a language together. Maybe you'd like to move to a new neighborhood, a new city, a new country! Just start dreaming a little as a couple. What are you looking forward to, *together?*

❖ We're going to suggest the two of you talk about this in the "Afterward" section, but it's best to begin the process of dreaming first by yourself. Just dream a little. How could adventure begin to come into your marriage?

THE CORE IDEAS

This session combines the key thoughts of chapters five and seven in *Love and War*. Those core ideas are:

• Companionship is far more the actual brick and mortar of two lives lived together. Companionship is the glue that allows a marriage to make it—not just through the hard times, but make it in the sense of finding your way to something rich together.

• Despite our vows, our hopes and dreams, most couples end up living separate lives.

• The two of you are part of something beautiful and dangerous. This is crucial to a Christian understanding of marriage. "We're in this together" is one of the strongest cords that binds two hearts together.

• There is a process we go through to enter into the mission of our marriage. Step one involves building companionship. Step two is to start dreaming together. Step three is to pray, "God, what do you have for us?" and also, "God, what are we involved in that we shouldn't be?"

GROUP TIME

Watch the session four video together. If you would like, use the following space to take notes on anything that stood out to you.

After watching the video, discuss as a group any or all of the following questions:

1. Let's start with a first reaction. What spoke to you in this week's chapters, or this video session?

2. Morgan and Cherie talked about how once the kids came, it seemed all the time they had for each other vanished. Craig and Lori admitted that even when he was a pastor, it felt like they were living separate lives, that Lori didn't really have a place in that. How has life gotten in and caused the two of you to live separate lives?

3. Bart and Tannah talked about a trip they shared to the Grand Canyon, how it fostered a sense of adventure in their marriage. Have you guys shared something like that in the past year?

4. How do you find adventure in your marriage?

5. John asked about mission—how you find that sense of "we're about something together." How do you experience that? Is mission a new idea for your marriage?

6. Craig said that living in a larger story, living together for something God is doing, has drawn him and Lori together. Do you experience that in your marriage?

7. In the teaching, John suggested that as couples we ask God two things: First, what he has for us by way of a shared mission. And second, what we are involved in that we shouldn't be. How can the two of you clear some time for each other, and for God? What shift can you make to begin to build adventure into your marriage, and find a mission together?

AFTERWARD

❖ What would you like to talk to your spouse about?

At the beginning of chapter seven, Stasi talked about our way of dreaming about the New Year. How we'll "take up pen and paper and write down—in a completely unedited fashion—all the things we'd love to do in the coming year. It's good for the heart to do some dreaming; it pulls you out of the rut, lifts your eyes to the horizon. We do the exercise first alone, then we come together to talk about our dreams and desires and to see what we might make happen." This would be a really good thing to do—dream a little on your own, and then come together and talk about those dreams.

We also suggested that the two of you begin to pray, "God, what do you have for us?"

And then keep your eyes and ears open for how God answers that prayer. Sometimes the adventure comes to us, as with a phone call after dinner that takes you to the side of a friend in need. For you know well enough by now that quite often adventure is something that finds us. As the children said in Narnia, "Let us take the adventure Aslan sends us." If you are even half awake with a pluck of courage in your heart, you'll soon find more adventure than you can handle. Which brings us to the other part of the prayer we should be praying: "God, what are we involved in that we *shouldn't* be?"

We must ask this as well, for we often find ourselves committed to things that God did *not* bring our way. People saddle us with their causes, family tends to assert its agenda, and soon we are buried in dramas that rob us of time and passion for the things God does have for us. Getting yourselves out of things you should not be involved in is crucial to finding the life God does have for you. Sometimes, he'll use misery and unhappiness to get you to move.

ACTIVITY:

In addition to talking about your dreams and desires, or, as the setting in which to talk about them, get out and adventure this week! Even something simple like checking out a new Chinese restaurant, or roller skating, or taking a drive to a new part of town or in the country. Get on your city paper's website and look up "events." There may be a concert in the park, or something else equally fun to do. Heck, go bowling!

This week, you'll want to do the "Personal Preparation" part for session five.

NOTES

SESSION

5

THE ENEMY IS NOT YOUR SPOUSE

We confessed earlier in the book our naïve view of the story when we got married. We thought the plot was, "Love God. Love each other. And everything will work out!" Our naïveté nearly cost us our marriage. We learned the hard way (do any of us ever really learn any other way?) that there is a whole lot more going on here. We had to face our brokenness. That was a shock. We had to confront our style of relating. That was humbling. We needed to learn that this is a far more dangerous story than we thought, that there is so much at stake. And maybe the biggest eye-opener of all—*we learned we had an enemy.*

PERSONAL PREPARATION

Read chapter six in *Love and War,* and answer the following questions.

❖ Start with a first reaction. (Often this is the very thing the Lord is using to speak to us.) What struck you in chapter six?

❖ I told the story of our twenty-fifth wedding anniversary, how we did slip away to Santa Fe, and the wonderful dinner we had (complete with Josh Groban on the radio!). How the next day, we were both "irritated" at each other. Can you relate to the story? Do you have a similar story to tell—how certain "feelings" creep in about your spouse, even on the heels of a good time together?

Back to the drama in the Garden of Eden.

Remember now, God gave us this story of the first marriage to help us get our bearings. It provides some very essential categories for navigating *our* marriages—like how gender is so fundamental to our identity, and how we were made for Paradise. How mankind fell and what that Fall did to our lives *as* men and women. And it also makes something else absolutely and utterly clear—we have an enemy.

Now there's a thought.

I mean, we all feel from time to time that we have an enemy, but the enemy feels like our spouse—right? Sometimes you just walk into the room and *see* them and they feel like the enemy. "One day out of three," a friend cynically said to me.

This chapter is about our Enemy, who is Satan. But far more often, especially during an argument or after some painful event, it is our spouse who feels like the "enemy." C'mon now—how much do you blame on your spouse, and how much do you actually blame on Satan?

You have an enemy. Your marriage has an enemy. Believe or not, this is very good news.

Because the epiphany that follows is this—your spouse is not the enemy. He is not the enemy. She is not the enemy. Really. "Sometimes we have to say that to each other, when things are getting heated," my friend Dan confessed. "I have to tell her, 'I am not the enemy. You are not the enemy.' Because it sure can feel that way." It sure can. For years Stasi and I lived with this constant feeling of accusation in our marriage. She "felt" accused by me, and I "felt" accused by her. What a relief it was to discover that these feelings of accusation were not actually ours; they were coming from him who is called "the Accuser" (Revelation 12:10).

❖ Can you relate to that feeling of being "accused" by your spouse (or dismissed, or that they are disappointed or angry with you), even just being in the same room? And where did you think that was coming from?

Dear friends, if this is not a category you think in, you will not understand your life and you will sure not understand what is happening in your marriage. If this is not an assumption you use to interpret daily thoughts, emotions, and events, you'll be as bamboozled as dear old Leslie. Pressed to choose our "top three things that would most help your marriage," we would come down to this list: (1) find life in God, (2) deal with your brokenness, and (3) learn to shut down the spiritual warfare that comes against your marriage. Practice this and nothing else, and you will be *amazed* at the freedom, love, and joy that will begin to flow.

❖ Is this a category you use in your day-to-day life, in your marriage? A good test of this would be, how often do you pray directly against Satan's schemes in your marriage? As a couple? And if the answer is "not that often," then who are you really blaming for all the conflict, tension, and disappointment?

We want to be as clear as possible what we mean by an "agreement."

Satan is a liar, "the father of lies" (John 8:44), so utterly convincing he deceived a glorious man and woman to betray God, whom they walked with every day. I think we tend to dismiss Adam and Eve as the idiots who got us all into this mess in the first place. But they had not yet sinned; they had experienced no wounding; they were man and woman in their glory. And they were deceived. It ought to give us all a healthy respect for what the enemy is capable of. Even the best of us can be taken in.

Now, what this father of lies does is put his "spin" on a situation. It typically comes as a "thought" or a "feeling." *She doesn't really love you. He'll never change. She's always doing that.* (By the way, when the word "always" is part of the equation, you know you are well into an agreement).

What Satan is hoping to secure from us is an agreement—that often very subtle but momentous shift in us where we *believe* the spin, we *go with* the feeling, we *accept* as reality the deception he is presenting. (It always *feels* so true.) *Just settle for what you've got* or *Don't risk being hurt again.*

❖ Are you aware of how the enemy is trying to get you to make "agreements" about your marriage? Can you see now that not every thought that passes through your head is your own?

So—this will be an absolute epiphany—ask Jesus. "Lord, what are the agreements I have been making about my marriage? What are the agreements that I've been making about love? What are the agreements I've been making about my spouse?"

Here are few sample agreements to help you name yours:

It's just not going to get any better.

Don't rock the boat—settle for what you've got.

It's not worth the effort, don't give it one more try.

Never let anyone hurt you again.

I'm just not going to trust her/him anymore.

You do your thing and I'll do mine.

I shouldn't have married him/her.

I'd be happier with someone else.

❖   Do this—ask Jesus right now to reveal to you the agreements you've been making about your marriage. About love. About your spouse. Pause, and listen. Sometimes Christ will reveal this to us in a "thought" that comes. Sometimes we'll simply feel the emotion we've felt around the agreement, feelings like *It isn't worth it,* or, *He doesn't love me.* Sometimes we'll even "hear" ourselves repeating the agreement. Or perhaps, we recall saying something to ourselves as we walk away from an argument with our spouse. Perhaps the list on page 63 can help you. Write down the agreements you've been making in each of these three categories:

My Marriage

Love

My Spouse

Now look at those agreements, and ask yourself, "What is the fruit of my making this agreement? What is the effect on me, and on my marriage?"

Now, as Christ reveals agreements to you, what you need to do is *break them*. You must renounce them.

> *Jesus, forgive me for giving place to this in my heart. I reject this agreement. I renounce it. I break agreement with*—[fill in the blank, what is it?]. *I break this agreement and I ask for your light and I ask for your love to come into these very places. Shine your light here. Bring me back to what is true. Bring your love into this place, Lord. In Jesus' name I pray. Amen.*

❖   Do this very thing. Right now! Break the agreements you are aware of. Do it out loud. Write your renouncement here if you like.

Now, we wish the enemy's work ended with agreements. But you know it doesn't. That's just the first pass, the first swipe he takes at the two of you. Why is it that over the past two years, every time a dear friend of ours sets out to lend his assistance on a church trip overseas—simply to play what many would see as a "background role"—his wife comes down with a terrible infection in her colon? An infection the doctors still do not understand, cannot diagnose, and cannot help to relieve? Is that coincidence? Why is it that every time Mary tries to recover sexual intimacy with her husband—something they've surrendered over the years—she has nightmares about being assaulted?

Why is it that every time Janet and Dave try to pray together, their boys get into a rip-roaring fight and somebody gets hurt? Why is it that when Steven begins to make some headway at work, his wife Becky spirals into one of her depressions and remains in that dark place for some time? For that matter, why did we lose a huge chunk of this very chapter as we were writing this book? The file simply disappeared. Irrecoverable. Coincidence?

❖ Think about what is hard in your marriage. How have you been interpreting that? Have you blamed your spouse? Yourself? Have you just accepted it with resignation? What about Satan—have you considered his part in it?

You can divide couples into two categories and, having done so, predict their future with some certainty. Those who enjoy sex, and those who don't. Those who are dealing with their brokenness, and those who are ignoring it. But the most telling division is this: those couples who understand we are at war and are allied against the enemy, and those who refuse for whatever reason to face the fact. I'll put my money on the warriors every time.

Why do certain subjects always result in arguments for the two of you? Why is it that when you bring up the topic of money—or sex, his mother, her mother, your brother, how much time you spend at work, how much weight he or she has put on, where to spend the holidays—it all blows up in your face? It feels booby-trapped. Yes, exactly, it is. You just stumbled into the enemy's camp; you have just uncovered where he is working.

Now, what will you do?

There comes a time where you must turn and face it. "Okay, this is real. We live in a love story set in a great war. The enemy is having a field day with me, my thoughts, my emotions or it's having a field day with our marriage. It's coming after our kids, it's wrecking family vacations or our friendships or relationships. We are going to deal with it."

And dealing with it means you pray directly against it. *You pray against it.* This would probably be a pretty good barometer—if you don't do this, oh, once a week, you're probably being naïve.

❖ Are you aware of how easy it is to do anything but actually face your enemy? Where are you *not* dealing directly with his attacks in your marriage these days? Where are you "dodging," and trying to ignore it or blame some other source?

Satan and his minions don't take days off; they have no holidays. Actually it will prove to be one of the most encouraging things for your prayer life because spiritual attack responds to prayer more quickly than just about anything else. Not super easy, not every time, but more noticeably than anything else. You will both be so encouraged.

How do we learn to do this? If we were just starting out, we'd pray together the "Daily Prayer" found in the back of the book *Love and War*. Thirty days of that and you will be amazed how much fog clears.

Do you and your spouse pray together against your true Enemy? Do you see now what might be getting in the way? Can you make a move toward a united front? If your spouse is on the "same page" as you, we suggest the two of you begin to pray the "Daily Prayer" together. If they are not, then begin to pray it on your own!

You have an enemy. Your marriage has an enemy. Believe it or not, this is very good news.

The reason this is "good news" is that SO much of what many couples face when it comes to tension, fights, disappointments, and historic pitfalls can actually be resolved—not by hours of bickering but by a few minutes of prayer against the enemy!

THE CORE IDEAS

This session corresponds to chapter six in *Love and War*. The key truths for this chapter are:

———∞———

- We live in a love story, set in the midst of war. This is the "war" part of the story. You have an enemy. Your marriage has an enemy.

- What Satan is hoping to secure from us is an "agreement"— that often very subtle but momentous shift in us where we *believe* his lies, we *accept* as reality the deception he is presenting.

- There comes a time where you must turn and face your enemy. And dealing with it means you pray directly against it! Break the agreements. Pray against the attack on your marriage—together, if at all possible.

- We can find our way back to the love story *if* we will confront the many ways the enemy is coming against our marriages!

GROUP TIME

Watch the session five video together. If you would like, use the following space to take notes on anything that stood out to you.

After watching the video, discuss as a group any or all of the following questions:

1. Because this session is about the Enemy, it's a pretty good bet this has been a hard week. Maybe even some tension in the car coming over? Has that been true? And, how did you handle it? Did you recognize the Enemy?

2. What spoke to you in this week's chapter, or this video session?

3. We live in a love story, set in the midst of war. The fact that our marriage has an enemy is such a crucial truth, but most couples have not been taught this. Do you operate with this assumption—that your marriage has an enemy and it's *not* your spouse?

4. Bart and Tannah's story, about running late and getting stuck in traffic, and all the agreements that rush in—"She's always doing this. Things will never change." Can you relate to that story? How does this happen in your marriage?

5. Cherie and Morgan told the story of almost losing a precious vacation because of the attack of the enemy. But they stopped, and prayed, and broke the agreements. Does that make sense to you? Is this something you can put into practice?

6. Lori said something very important—that some of these lies and agreements have been a part of our marriage for so long, they become strongholds. It feels like a part of the marriage, and things will never change. So it takes a real act of will to break those long-standing agreements. Are you aware of what those are for the two of you?

7. Would it help if we prayed together to break those agreements? (You can stop, and be real specific about the things that have been shared. "Janet, why don't you start by renouncing that agreement, and we will join you in prayer." Let folks renounce their agreements, and then pray for one another!)

Consider praying the following prayer together before closing this session:

Lord Jesus, come and fill our marriages with your love and with your life. Flood our lives with your truth; shed light on those agreements we've been making about our spouse, or ourselves, or our marriage. Come, Spirit of God, and lead us into the truth. We renounce every one of those agreements now, in the name of Jesus Christ. We take our stand against the Enemy, and we reject his schemes against our marriages. We invite the life of God and the kingdom of God to fill our marriages, and to fill our hearts and minds toward one another. In Jesus' name.

AFTERWARD

❖ What would you like to talk to your spouse about?

WARNING: The topic of the enemy is booby-trapped. This is the LAST thing he wants the two of you coming to clarity about, and taking a united stand against. So head's up—this is a ripe time for "arguments" and "tensions" and "misunderstandings." Do not run with it. Do not make a whole new round of agreements!

"Honey, what struck you tonight? Did the Lord say something to you?"

Read the story of "Ken and Macey" (found in chapter six of the book *Love and War*) together, out loud. Then ask your spouse, "Honey, how can I do this for you?"

ACTIVITY:

Pray the "Daily Prayer" (found in the back of the book *Love and War*) together for several days. Stasi and I will take a paragraph at a time, and pray it out loud together.

But let's not make this all about the "war" side of the story. Get out and do something fun this week!

This week, you'll want to do the "Personal Preparation" part for session six.

NOTES

NOTES

SESSION

6

STORM CLOUDS

When crisis hits and something shakes us to our foundation, we all start grasping, clutching, looking for someone to blame or some place to hold on. Like people do when they're drowning. Panic overcomes us; we rush to blame or speculation or a box of doughnuts. Before you make another move, you need to ask yourself: *Why* is it hard right now?

Don't jump to conclusions. Your *interpretation* of what's going on will shape everything that follows—your emotions, your perspective, and your decisions.

PERSONAL PREPARATION

Read chapter ten in *Love and War*, and answer the following questions.

❖ Was there something that leapt out at you, something that got your attention in this chapter? And why do you think that got your attention?

Earlier, in chapter three, we wrote this:

Stasi and I were talking about marriages we know, and we came to a pretty sobering realization—we can't name one single marriage that hasn't been through deep waters in the last three years. Not one. And we know a lot of people, and therefore a lot of marriages. Between family, friends, church, work, and the neighborhood, you'd think we'd be able to point to some couple who is trouble free. We can't find one. *Not one.* Every single marriage we know is either currently struggling, or they've just passed through some major struggle, or they've thrown in the towel.

❖   Hard times are part of every marriage. Let's just pause, and admit this fact. It's not just you. How does this truth help you?

❖   Are the two of you going through a hard time right now? Or have you been through a hard time in your past? What was it all about? (Hard times aren't necessarily crises; they might be distance and separation between you, or they might be the lingering deep disappointments you have in your marriage.)

Two nights ago, Stasi was in an accident. She called to ask me what to do. I am ashamed to admit how quickly I started jumping to conclusions. I wanted to blame her for going too fast; I wanted to chastise her for not using four-wheel drive. Good grief. My poor wife is standing out in the cold, shaken, asking me for help and I'm leaping to accusation like a prosecuting attorney.

When crisis hits and something shakes us to our foundation, we all start grasping, clutching, looking for someone to blame or some place to hold on. Like people do when they're drowning. Panic overcomes us; we rush to blame or speculation or a box of doughnuts. Before you make another move, you need to ask yourself, *why* is it hard right now?

Don't jump to conclusions. Don't start making unexamined agreements. *We're going down. He doesn't love me. It's my fault. We should never have gotten married.* Slow down for a second. Your *interpretation* of what's going on will shape everything that follows—your emotions, your perspective, and your decisions. If you are mistaken, you will wander way off course and pay a great price. Take a deep breath; put down the gun; ask yourself, *Why* is it hard? What is this about?

❖ How *have* you been interpreting the hard times? Can you relate to "jumping to conclusions"? Do you tend to blame, or go to fear, or speculation—or resignation?

On pages 160 through 164 of the *Love and War* book, we named six categories that are helpful for interpreting hard times in a marriage. Take a moment to think about these:

Transformation—Whatever else might be going on, you know God is using your marriage to make you holy. You also know by now that the log in your own eye makes it hard to see anything clearly. So even if the primary cause for the crisis lies beyond you, it's best to start here.

❖ What is God after in your own life these days? Are you aware of the transformation still needed in your own character? What is the "log" in your own eye that you need to look at first?

Warfare—You live in a world at war. Spiritual attack *must* be a category you think in, or you will misunderstand more than half of what happens in your marriage.

❖ What is the Enemy up to in your marriage these days? Warfare is almost always a factor. How might Satan be involved—either by causing the hard times or, by trying to make them worse in getting you to make agreements? *Are* you making agreements?

Brokenness—Sometimes the craziness in our marriage comes from deep brokenness in us or in our spouse. But we're so embarrassed by it we try to hide it as long as we can. So God uses troubles to flush us out of hiding.

❖ Can you see brokenness playing itself out in your marriage? What is your brokenness? What is your spouse's? How is this brokenness affecting the marriage?

Seasons—Marriage has its ebbs and flows; that's just the way it is. There will be times when you are close, and times when you couldn't feel farther apart. For no other reasons than that's just the way these things go. People have their ebbs and flows, too. If one of you is walking through a dark valley personally, of course it affects the marriage. But it's not *about* the marriage. This is really quite relieving.

❖ Is it possible that the hard times might just be a season? Have you talked to God about this?

The World—How many arguments happen for no other reason than you're both tired? How many times is "sexual disinterest" not an issue of lost attraction, but simply exhaustion? The question is, *Why* are we so tired? Has the world crept in and stolen the life from us? *Jesus, is there something about the way we live that needs to change?*

❖ Has the pace of life, or stress, or crisis outside the marriage played a role in where the two of you are right now?

Perseverance—Hope is a fruit of proven character; proven character is forged through persevering during times of suffering. Some hard times are simply for our good. There are certain things you never discover about God until you go through hard times; there are things you never discover about yourself, too. And so it is good to ask God, *Father, is this from your hand? Is this simply something you are asking me to endure?*

❖ Some hard times are pointing to real issues that must be dealt with in the marriage, or brokenness that must be dealt with in you or your spouse. But sometimes, it is something we must simply endure. What would perseverance require of you these days? What would it address in your character?

I'd [John] become so completely accustomed to my way of life I had no real idea its effect on others. What the group began to dismantle that day was my perfectionism, my guardedness, my resolve never to need anyone. They didn't trust me because I didn't trust them. Or anyone, for that matter. It was a very painful experience. I was the emperor and I was buck naked alright. But it set me on a journey toward change, and there has been no greater recipient of the blessing of that change than Stasi. I'm sad to say I never heard her attempts to address my impact on her; so God brought me through that program as a sort of end-run to get to me.

You have to own what is yours to own in the troubles of your marriage.

You also have to insist that your spouse face themselves as well.

It is not love to ignore your spouse's sin, or brokenness, or immaturity. It is not love to let something wrong carry on. It is not right. Truth be told, it is a *lack of love* that lets it all go on for years. When we let our own fears keep us from bringing something up with our spouse, that is self-protection.

Or indifference. God loves until what he loves is pure.

❖ This would be a very good thing to try to name, and write down. What do you need to "own" as *your* part in the troubles of your marriage? And what does your spouse need to own?

81

❖ And what, then, does love look like—if love does not allow things to go on ignored? What steps must you take?

THE CORE IDEAS

This session corresponds to chapter ten in *Love and War*. The key ideas in this chapter are:

— ⊗⊗⊗ —

• Hard times come to every marriage. Don't let this throw you.

• How we interpret hard times is crucial. Don't jump to conclusions. Don't start making unexamined agreements. Your *interpretation* of what's going on will shape everything that follows—your emotions, your perspective, and your decisions.

• Scripture gives us any number of reasons for rough waters; each of them requires a *different response.*

• Love is insistent. Love moves toward a resolution.

• There is healing; there is hope.

GROUP TIME

Watch the session six video together. If you would like, use the following space to take notes on anything that stood out to you.

After watching the video, discuss as a group any or all of the following questions:

1. Let's start with a first reaction. What spoke to you in this week's chapter, or this video session?

2. This is a tough one—talking about hard times in our marriages. Partly because we are all in different places. Some of us might be in a wonderful season of marriage right now; some of us might have just passed through a hard time; some might be in a really tough time right now. Have you guys seen some rough waters in your marriage? What was it about?

3. One of the crucial points John and Stasi spoke on was "Don't jump to conclusions! There are different reasons for hard times; each requires a different response!" John confessed wanting to blame Stasi for getting into the accident. Cherie said she felt she and Morgan had reached a point where God could no longer redeem the situation. When things are hard in your marriage, where do your thoughts and emotions tend to go?

4. Craig and Lori talked about the recent cancer, and how it was affecting them. How sometimes hard things pull us apart from one another. How do you typically handle hard times—do you isolate, or pull together?

5. Here is a critical sentence from chapter ten: "There are certain things you never discover about God until you go through hard times; there are things you never discover about yourself, too." Morgan said he could see God using the hard times to get to something deeper in his life as well as Cherie's. What has God used your hard times to bring to the surface in you, or in your marriage?

6. And how did you respond to what God surfaced?

7. What have you learned about God through hard times?

8. Chapter ten ended with the story Jesus told about the two houses—one built on sand, the other on the rock. The storms hit both houses, but only one stood. What do you hold onto in the storm? What truths have seen you through the hard times?

AFTERWARD

❖ What would you like to talk to your spouse about?

WARNING: Remember what we said about timing: timing is *everything* in marriage. If you need to bring up some difficult matters with your spouse, make sure you are praying beforehand. Pray that it goes well; ask a friend to be praying with you. AND, ask Jesus *how* to bring it up, and *when.*

If your marriage is going through hard times right now, this would be a good time for the two of you to see a Christian counselor. Are you open to that? (Ask your friends for a referral. Or, check the "Allies Network" at ransomedheart.com. The American Association of Christian Counselors also has a database of counselors.)

If you are in a hard time, or you know there are hard things for the two of you to talk about, use the six categories you journaled about in this section as a starting point; share with one another what you think is going on in each of those categories. It will help you see what is really the cause, and how to move forward from there.

One of the most crucial things to see you both through hard times is the knowledge that neither of you is going to leave the marriage. Your vows may be the only thing that keeps you from leaving some days, but that is partly their purpose. The assurance that neither you nor your spouse is going to jump ship is crucial to finding your way through the storm. SO, it would be a powerful thing to sit down together, and say that to one another: "I am never going to leave you. I am committed to our marriage. I intend to keep my vows."

This week, you'll want to do the "Personal Preparation" part for session seven.

NOTES

SESSION

7

SEX

Fight for a sexual life with your spouse that is frequent, and deeply satisfying for both of you. Take risks. Offer strength, offer beauty. Be vulnerable, be fully present. That is the way of love, *especially* in a time of war. As God said, drink deeply, O lovers.

PERSONAL PREPARATION

For this week, read chapter eleven in *Love and War*, and answer the following questions.

❖ It is always good to start with a first reaction. What struck you in this chapter's discussion of sex?

When we started mapping out this book, we knew we wanted to speak to the issues entangled with sex. But now that we are here, we're having second thoughts. *Dear Lord, we're going to include a chapter on sex? What in heaven's name do we say? What stories do we tell?* We decided to keep the whole chapter to three lines:

You need to do it. Often. In a way you both enjoy it. Immensely.

If this isn't the case, then you need to deal with why it isn't. Because you need to do it. Often. In a way you both enjoy it. Immensely.

We were only partly joking, but why the need to make jokes? What are we all so nervous about? What is it about sex that makes it the most awkward thing to talk about—one of the classic "no fly zones"—even among couples who've been married for years? (Do you two talk about your sex life much? With ease?)

❖ Do you? If the truth is, "not really," *why* not? Are there things you would like to talk to your spouse about regarding your sex life?

There are three things that are too amazing for me,
four that I do not understand:
the way of an eagle in the sky,
the way of a snake on a rock,
the way of a ship on the high seas,
and the way of a man with a maiden (Proverbs 30:18–19).

The author is trying to explore the mystery of sex, and using *poetry* to do it (which is probably the only way; no technical manuals here). Did you notice the connections? An eagle in the sky, high and lifted up, rising above the earth. Sex is transcendent. Sex helps us to rise above the petty, the little foxes; in fact for sex to be good we *have to* transcend ourselves as we love one another. Which is one of its greatest gifts—to be free, if but a moment, from that constant self-consciousness that besets mankind. Sex ought to lift you above yourself; it ought to be soaring.

A snake on a rock is usually warming itself, soaking in the rays of the sun and the heat radiating from the earth. The poem takes us from the transcendent to the earthy. It's hot and sweaty. Often Stasi and I draw close to one another and lie there warming ourselves to each other, warming to our bodies again, warming to the act. And when the snake begins to move, it is graceful and undulating.

Then the writer uses the metaphor of a ship on the high seas. Holy cow, these Bible guys really got it right. Sex as a storm. Sex as a ship carried along by a tempest—waves crashing over the decks, all hands holding on for dear life. We are meant to be swept up into it, carried along by its power and majesty. There is no such thing as "safe" sex; this is not something you can control nor do you really want to (though Lord knows in our fear and woundedness we do try and control it). The surging power of sex ought to humble us, unnerve us, cause us to want to learn its ways like sailors so that we can at least trim our sails, turn our bows into the oncoming waves, make the most of the careening ride. To be foolish with sex is to risk violence and destruction (that's where the stern commands come in). But after the storm has passed, we feel a sense of awe, of worship even.

❖ How do these three metaphors, these poetic expressions of sexual intimacy, help you think about your sexual intimacy? Take each of the three and ask yourself, *Is this what our sex is like?* And, more importantly, *Is this what I* want *it to be like?*

Transcendent

Earthy

Tempestuous

Marriage is the sanctuary God created for sex, and only there, in the refuge of covenantal love, will you find sex at its best. For a lifetime. The coming together of two bodies in the sensual fireworks of sex is meant to be a *consummating* act, the climactic event of two hearts and souls that have already been coming together outside the bedroom and can't wait to complete the intimacy as deeply as they possibly can. "I *want* you," says it all. The passion comes from the soul; the opening movements of this symphony take place well before there are four bare legs in bed.

So let's begin here—sex when there is love is the best sex of all. Giving sex without love borders on prostitution; demanding sex without love is abuse. We're talking about the intertwining of two *hearts* as their bodies become one. The more you have that in mind, the better things will go.

❖ Does your sexual intimacy with your spouse feel like the consummation of a heart-to-heart intimacy? If not, what is in the way of the heart-to-heart intimacy?

I've counseled many married women who have told me, "I'll give him my body. But not my soul." The reason being that "he" has not won the right to enter her soul, and I would argue he has therefore not won the right to enter her body. When a woman opens herself up for her man it is an act of stunning vulnerability. This kind of inviting openness can only be won through love and trust. God thus builds into the sexual mystery an *insistence* upon love and trust outside of bed. How true to his character; it does not work to come to God for the "goodies"—answered prayers, blessings of whatever sort—apart from relationship with him. The treasures are for those who love him, and *live* like it. So it is with a woman.

❖ Ladies—do you relate to the vow, "I'll give him my body, but not my soul"? What would it require of you to offer your heart *and* soul to your husband in bed?

While we are speaking of Eve, notice that God also creates her sexuality in such a way that she often—not always, but often—has a sexual crescendo that requires more time than her man's. He is a stick of dynamite; she is a geyser. He has a short fuse and then wow; she builds and builds and then hallelujah. Why would God do this? Why introduce more frustration into an already tenuous and awkward environment? The stark contrast in our arousal and orgasm must have some design to it. This, too, is absolutely beautiful. There's no wham-bam-thank-you-ma'am allowed. What is God asking of a man when he creates Eve's sexuality in such a way that Adam can't just "do it"? There is a holding back for him, a wooing and loving and foreplay so that she can be as fully enrapt as he wants to be.

How utterly lovely—it requires unselfishness on his part.

❖ Guys—how selfish does your sexual fulfillment seem to you? Do you honor your wife's different sexual needs, and arousal? What would it look like for you to be more loving of your wife's feminine heart, when it comes to having sex with her?

The beauty of Adam's sexuality is that it requires Eve to come out of hiding, too. Men typically want sex more often than their woman (though none of these are hard and fast rules; we are speaking in general terms which have proven true down through history). Men want sex more often and they are more "ready" for it than their woman. What does this require of Eve? That we take risks, that we come out of our comfort zone. Most women hide in busyness and efficiency; every last one of us doubts we have a beauty to offer. And so to offer ourselves to our man requires love and courage, requires us to put him first even as our sexuality asks him to put us first.

❖ Ladies—what would it look like for you to sexually come out of hiding toward your husband?

Many things go into a good marriage, but at the core it is essentially Strength and Beauty. This goes way beyond sex. It is a reality which permeates every aspect of our lives as men and women.

This all plays itself out in hundreds of ways before we ever jump between the sheets. A man offers strength when he simply engages at the end of his day; he turns off ESPN and turns to his wife—"How are you? Tell me about your day." I cancel a meeting, invite Stasi to go out to breakfast; it makes her day. (These things don't have to be dramatic). A man engages when he protects his wife from a controlling mother: "She's not available right now. She'll call in a couple days." And when he provides a place for her emotions—without being consumed by them, and offering tender understanding.

When a man goes passive, it is a compromise of his very essence. And it hurts the people around him. He can starve his wife by refusing to talk to her; he can make her feel utterly abandoned by refusing to engage in her life. That is why a man loves a woman by offering his strength.

❖ Guys—where and how are you offering your strength to your wife these days? And, where might you be starving her of your engagement?

❖ And fellas—what did you think of the late-night story I told of rescuing Stasi by fighting for her? What did that stir in you?

A woman offers beauty when she offers kindness. The world does not provide tenderness or mercy on a regular basis and we all need it. Offering your husband a safe harbor for his thoughts, concerns, or doubts, and not giving way to fear yourself is a beautiful expression of your love. Seeing your husband's strength and telling him what you see feeds his soul. One of the most priceless gifts a woman can give her husband is the message that she believes in him; he is the real deal; he is a real man. We offer our beauty when we do not fear his masculinity or our femininity. Wearing a pretty nightgown is just one tangible picture of embracing both. For a woman to wear a piece of lingerie feels exceedingly risky. Exactly. It is vulnerable. Letting down your guard and offering your tender vulnerability to your husband conveys a message to him of beauty beyond words.

When a woman goes hard, it is a compromise of her very essence. And it hurts the people around her. She can emasculate her man through her controlling efficiency, her refusal to be vulnerable. She can starve her husband through her busyness and unavailability. That is why a woman loves a man by offering her beauty.

❖ Ladies—where and how are you offering your beauty and vulnerability to your husband these days? And where might you be depriving him?

❖ And ladies—what did you think of Stasi's story about the nightgown, and taking the risk of offering the beauty she did have? What did that stir in you?

LOVE & WAR PARTICIPANT'S GUIDE

The son of man came to seek and save what was lost. The hopefulness of this promise is like a sunrise. Even as I [John] read it again, having read it many times before, something in my heart quiets down a bit; the clamoring and fear subside. God is about restoring the very things I care about, too.

What a relief. We've got big help on our side. He knows something about resurrection.

We live in a love story set in the midst of a terrible war. So it should not come as a surprise that our sexuality is often a place of disappointment, sorrow, and loss. Maybe *the* place. The enemy specializes in wreaking havoc with human sexuality; when he wounds a man or woman here, he wounds them about as deeply as they can be wounded. So don't be surprised when your sexual intimacy is opposed; the sanctity of the marriage bed is a war zone. Before marriage, desire and passion don't seem to be a problem—well, keeping them in check is the problem. But often after the vows the passion turns to fear, the desire to hesitation. It's not just your marriage; it's everyone's. Because we are broken people with often very broken pasts, it can be hard to find consistent, abandoned sexual joy in marriage. But much can be recovered, much can be healed.

❖ Now that we have reached chapter ten, do you see the reality of the great "war" playing itself out in your love story—especially in your sexuality? How does this help you interpret the rough times and awkwardness you may hit in your sexual intimacy?

Talk about it. Talk about your sexual life together. Ask your spouse how they are feeling about sex with you, what they enjoy, what they would love to see happen. Most times I'm a little shy even to let Stasi see me naked and sexually aroused—it just feels so vulnerable. For years we didn't really talk about our sexuality. But it has been good to venture there—to ask, "How was last night for you?" and, "What do you enjoy?" and even, "Can I tell you why I haven't seemed interested lately?"

Talking about it disarms speculation, the playground of the enemy. It also requires you to sort through your own feelings about your sexuality, which is a very good thing to do. Neglect leaves room for the cobwebs and spiders to move in. Your heart needs to be fully engaged here—if it's not, you want to know why not.

❖ What would you want to talk to your spouse about regarding your sexuality? This is a good thing to do "Afterward," but you'll want to give it some thought here.

Then pray about it. Invite Christ into your sexuality, into your marriage bed. We *had* to do this for years, because our past was hanging over the moment like dark clouds. At first we each prayed privately, not even knowing the other was praying; then we grew to the place where we could pray openly about it together. This has been absolutely incredible for us. Just this week I was feeling that there was too much distance between us, too much awkwardness. Stasi had been experiencing some physical discomfort when we made love; I let the enemy use it to accuse me. But I prayed that Jesus would come and restore our lovemaking, that he would fill it with his grace. Once again, he did.

❖ How often do you pray for the richness and blessing of God in your sexual intimacy? Are you motivated now to pray far more passionately about your sex life?

"What I wish he knew ..." Ladies, how would you fill in the rest of that? What I want to say to John is this—it's all foreplay. The tone of your voice. The look in your eye. The gentle pat on the back as you pass by me. The way you cleared the table and dove in to help with the dishes. Your laughter. Sitting down next to me and asking me how I'm doing ... what have I been thinking about. Reading aloud to me the part in the book that moved you. The tiny ways you convey you enjoy me. Baby, that's it. My heart is yours. So now, in the bedroom, I'm all yours as well.

❖ Write out your thoughts here—"What I wish my husband knew ..."

"What I wish she knew ..." Men, what is it you wish your wife knew? What I want to say to Stasi is this—where is that negligee? Wear it more often. I love it when you initiate. Wake me up in the night if you want to. I love it when you make me feel like the hero during the day, when you say to me "Honey, you are amazing." I want to know what pleases you; I want to know that *I* please you.

❖ Write out your thoughts here—"What I wish my wife knew ..."

Now, many of you were sexually active before marriage. Stasi and I both were, and it breaks my heart to say so. There is nothing glorious about it whatsoever, no matter what Hollywood might say. It does such damage. You have to deal with the past in order to take hold of your future. I was introduced to pornography in the third grade. Stasi was sexually abused when she was young; she was raped as a woman of nineteen. Both of us experienced the sorrow of abortion. More than once. You've got to remember this love story is assaulted by evil. But if we can find our way out of such pain, darkness, and sin to a sexuality that is richer and better than ever before, then you can, too.

You *will* have to fight for healing and breakthrough; this doesn't just show up with the mail. The good news is, healing and breakthrough are available. Some of that we found through counseling; some we found through healing prayer. Some came as we fought the Enemy, and some came simply as we chose to love one another.

We've included a prayer for sexual healing in the back of the *Love and War* book that many people have found very, very helpful. Set aside some time to pray through it!

THE CORE IDEAS

- God has created the human form and the human heart to experience passion and ecstasy—transcendent, earthy, and tempestuous—when we are fully loving one another. It is a gift he intended us to enjoy. Often.

- The coming together of two bodies in the sensual fireworks of sex is meant to be a *consummating* act, the climactic event of two hearts and souls that have already been coming together outside the bedroom and can't wait to complete the intimacy as deeply as they possibly can.

- The sexual act is a stunning picture of what a man and woman essentially offer one another in every aspect of life. It is a metaphor, a passion play on what it means to be masculine and feminine.

- All this is to say, ladies and gentlemen, that if it doesn't feel risky you are probably playing it safe.

> • Because we are broken people with often very broken pasts, it can be hard to find consistent, abandoned sexual joy in marriage. But much can be recovered, much can be healed. And it is worth fighting for.

GROUP TIME

Watch the session seven video together. If you would like, use the following space to take notes on anything that stood out to you.

After watching the video, discuss as a group any or all of the following questions:

1. Let's start with a first reaction. What spoke to you in this week's chapter, or this video session?

2. Lori and Tannah both talked about how agreements here, in sexuality, have such an impact. Lori said, "When deep-seated agreements are there, it keeps you from loving one another." Can you relate? Can you name what some of those agreements might be?

3. Morgan and Cherie talked about how once the kids came, sex went out the window, simply because as young parents they are exhausted all the time. What else gets in the way of intimacy, including sexual intimacy?

4. One of the key ideas here is that what happens outside the bedroom shapes what happens in the bedroom. That as men, we offer strength, and as women, we offer beauty. The ladies talked about what they enjoy from their men, what brings romance, and how they love to be pursued. What did you connect with in what they shared?

5. And ladies, what do you love your husband to do when he pursues you?

6. The guys did the same, talked about how they love to experience their wives offering tenderness and beauty, what they find arousing. What did you connect with in what the men shared?

7. And guys, what do you love your wife to do, when she offers you her femininity?

8. Morgan shared how he and Cherie are trying to cultivate intimacy in other areas of their life together—intellectual intimacy, emotional intimacy, spiritual intimacy. Where would you love to develop and deepen your intimacy in these other areas as husband and wife?

AFTERWARD

❖ What would you like to talk to your spouse about?

In the chapter, and in your journaling here in the guide, you were given the chance to think about "What I wish he knew/What I wish she knew." Share your thoughts and desires with one another.

Notice that the seductress in movies is often the "helpless" woman who makes the man feel like a man. "I think you are amazing," she says with a bat of her eyes and the signal that she's all his, and bam—he's hooked.

Notice that the gigolo in movies is always the man who wants to talk to her, wants to know her feelings, makes her feel beautiful. "You are the most beautiful woman in the world," he says, "and I would do anything for you." Bam, she's hooked.

Ladies, how can you tell your man you think he is amazing?

Guys, how can you tell your woman you think she is beautiful?

ACTIVITY:

Ummm ... are suggestions really needed for this week's "activity"? (wink, wink).

This week, you'll want to do the "Personal Preparation" part for session eight.

NOTES

SESSION

8

A THOUSAND LITTLE CHOICES

I think we all look for love to come in dramatic ways. We know love is powerful and beautiful—how come it doesn't *feel* like it? Love plays itself out in what seems like such unremarkable ways—you pick up your socks, you ignore their snarky comment, you put the toilet seat down. But this is exactly what makes it epic—the fact that love plays itself out in a thousand little choices, unseen and *without* supporting soundtrack. That's what makes it so beautiful.

PERSONAL PREPARATION

This is your last week! Read chapter twelve in *Love and War*, and answer the following questions.

❖ It is always good to start with a first reaction. What struck you in chapter twelve?

There are couples who find their way to something beautiful. Truly beautiful. We pray that you will be among them.

And we believe if you will embrace the help offered here and stick with it for more than a couple of weeks—more than you stick with your diets or exercise or savings plans—you have a much higher chance of joining those who have found their way to a beautiful and powerful marriage. But there is no guarantee, of course. You know that as well. So why bother? Why risk it? Why throw yourself wholeheartedly into such a dangerous, costly, and uncertain enterprise?

Measure your answer carefully.

❖ How would you answer that question now? First off, *are* you willing to throw yourself wholeheartedly into your marriage? Why, or why not?

This might be a good place to pause, and ask God's help with your commitment to your marriage:

Lord Jesus, I do—I give myself wholeheartedly first and foremost to you. You are my Life, and I belong to you. I commit myself now, by your grace, to a wholehearted engagement in my marriage. Give me your grace to live like you do, in my marriage. I renounce halfheartedness. I renounce fear, and resignation, and self-protection. I choose to give myself to my spouse and my marriage. Wholeheartedly. By the strength of your life within me. And in your name. Amen.

We're not trying to be discouraging; we're trying to be realistic. This is a love story, set in the midst of war. Marriage is a crucible; the gladiatorial arena for love and war. It will eventually expose every broken place in you; it will reveal your every sin, if only before the watching heavens. Your commitment to self-protection will be confronted daily. You will be disappointed and you will be wounded. You will most certainly be *tested*; there may not be a greater test of character on the planet. It begs the question—why in heaven's name would anyone throw themselves wholeheartedly into such a dangerous, costly, and uncertain enterprise?

"Because that is the kind of person I want to be."

Now that is a very good answer.

❖ Is this how you would answer the question? Why, or why not?

Because love is what we are created for; it is the reason for our existence. Love is our destiny. Love God and love one another—these are the two great commands upon the human race. The secret to life is this—we are here in order to learn how to love. It's really quite an epiphany when the truth finally strikes home. It might be the most liberating realization we ever come to. We are here in order to learn how to love. It is our greatest mission of all, our destiny.

This is the secret to life. How does that idea strike you now?

Though it is the most basic of truths, this epiphany seems to come to few of us—or rather, seems to be *accepted* by few of us. Most people remain committed to other things as their primary aim in life—happiness, survival, revenge, success, what have you.

❖ Think of the people you know—your family, your friends. What would you say they are living for, throwing their energy into? And is it working for them? And what about you—what would you say you are living for these days? What are you throwing your thoughts, time, and energy into? And how is it going?

But I [John] think you can fairly easily sort out the people who have come to this epiphany from those who haven't. There is something different about their approach to life—what upsets them, what makes them laugh, and *especially* the way they handle people. These folks may not have named it, but a shift has taken place. It nearly always comes through a painful disruption of some sort. They discover that their style of relating is an absolute disaster; they might have lost someone dear to them. Sometimes it comes with illness, the shock that their days really are numbered and what will they live for now? The epiphany might arrive—as in my case—through a revelation of their own utter selfishness. It most often comes through some kind of encounter with God. He lives to love and, if you hang around Jesus long enough, it rubs off on you.

However it may be delivered, the epiphany is the realization that life comes down to this, and this alone: We are here to love.

This is the great shift, the most fundamental realignment of our heart's ambitions. It strikes at the very core of sin in us. It is not a dismal thing at all.

Those who have made the shift are among the world's most joyful people. They are truly free.

❖ Do you know people like this—people who seem truly free to love? What are they like?

❖ And what is it that makes *you* upset these days; what makes you laugh; how do you handle people?

No matter what you are told ahead of time about marriage, it doesn't matter one bit till you are *in* it, till you have lived *within* marriage for some time. Then you begin to understand. It's sort of like trying every key on a large ring of keys to see which one will open the Door to Life. This one labeled "My spouse will make me happy" doesn't seem to work. The pretty one called "Happy little home" doesn't work either. The gnarled one named "Protect yourself" doesn't fit. Well I'll be doggoned—there's only one key here that opens the door, and it's this one—I am here to learn how to love.

Huh. It's the last key most of us try.

But it opens the door alright, and then we can get on with actually living our lives.

❖ What "key" would you say you have been trying to use in your marriage? Has it been successful?

I think we all look for love to come in dramatic ways. We know love is powerful and beautiful—how come it doesn't *feel* like it? Love plays itself out in what seems like such unremarkable ways—you pick up your socks, you ignore their snarky comment, you put the toilet seat down. But this is exactly what makes it epic—the fact that love plays itself out in a thousand little choices, unseen and *without* supporting soundtrack. That's what makes it so beautiful.

I'll run to the store. We can watch your show. Yes, you can dim the lights. No, I don't mind if you go out tonight. Would you like a little of my cookie? We meet these moments every day. This morning, we had to get down to an event for which we were the keynote speakers. Stasi and I agreed last night we'd better leave the house at eight. It is now ten after and she's not ready; she's futzing in the bathroom. It's moments like these that reveal what fuels us. *Hey, you were the one who said eight. Let's go.* Why am I tweaked? What's with the compulsion, the anxiousness? Isn't it really about wanting to get on top of things, making sure we make a good impression? It is godless; I'm thinking about my reputation, not my wife's heart.

So, I sat at the kitchen table and finished my oatmeal, had a cup of tea. I simply waited until she came out and said, "I'm ready." I didn't even get in that little dig men savor—"Finally." These are the little choices we are making every day. We are learning to love.

❖ What are the little choices you can begin making to show your spouse you love them? Try to name five, just as a way of getting yourself thinking about these things.

I [John] was asking Jesus the other day, "What do our readers need, Lord? What do their marriages need?" He said, *Healing.* So I asked, "How is the healing going to come?" And he said, *Forgiveness.* If there's to be an awakening of hope and desire, if there are to be some new frontiers in your relationship where you can talk about difficult things or you can handle conflict differently or approach sex differently, it is going to come through forgiveness.

We've done a lot of damage over the years.

All of us.

It will be the dawning of a new day and a very healing moment as we begin to ask forgiveness of one another. Simply to sit down together and say, "I know what I need to ask forgiveness for" (if you do), or simply to ask, "What's it like to live with me? What has the effect of my style of relating been on you over the years? Has it caused you to lose hope in certain areas of our life? I really want to know and I really need your forgiveness." That would be so extraordinarily healing.

I did this just last week. I was so aware—again—of how my self-protective style of relating, my "never need anyone" approach to life has hurt Stasi. We were driving home from somewhere, and I just felt moved to bring it up. I said, "Honey, I want to ask your forgiveness for not letting you in, for resolving never to need anyone. I'm so sorry. Please forgive me." (You see, we too are learning as we work our way through the things we've talked about in this book!)

❖　What do you need to ask forgiveness for? And how will you approach your spouse to ask this forgiveness?

Every time we choose to love, we take a step closer to God; it's like he's right there. Every time we choose something else, we take a step away.

I want God, so I choose love.

Don't get me wrong—I love Stasi, more than ever. Sometimes it scares me how much I love her, because my heart feels so utterly out there, so entirely vulnerable. You step out that far and you know you are opening yourself up for hurt. "Love anything," C. S. Lewis says, "and your heart will be wrung and possibly broken." *Possibly* being an understatement. Then we read the Scriptures telling us to love one another "as God loved us," and if you hadn't made the connection yet, that trail leads to a crown of thorns.

Pardon the grammar, but it don't come easy. Falling in love is how God gives us a push in the right direction. But then we have to choose. And we are going to need a very compelling reason to lay down our lives, day after day, year after year. To make those thousand little choices, for the thousand-and-oneth little time. Something needs to *compel* us.

What could be more compelling than this? When we abandon ourselves to love, we find ourselves closer to the One who is always doing that himself.

We find God.

LOVE & WAR PARTICIPANT'S GUIDE

❖ How does this strike you? Does it sound attractive? Is this the life you want? Let your heart give an unedited response.

We live in a love story, set in the midst of war. Love is our destiny, and all hell is set against it. Really, it explains so much. We wake each morning and find that we have to fight our way back to all that is true, fight off the thousand reasons to settle for less than the life we were created for. Our bodies awaken but then our hearts and souls must awaken, too, so that we might play our part in the Grand Affair. And God has made our hearts in such a way that nothing awakens us quite like some great mission which is ours alone to fulfill. Thus the power of fairy tales, all of which turn on this awakening in the heart on the boy and girl.

I expect this year will hold a number of battles; I imagine we'll face down many demons together. We'll probably worry unnecessarily about our sons. Despite our best intentions, I'll leave my clothes piled on the floor and Stasi will tell me where to turn. I'm also looking forward to all the joys that lie ahead; we laugh a lot these days. I'm hoping we make it back to the Tetons, and maybe even to Italy.

❖   We live in a love story, set in the midst of war. How is this shaping your perspective of life these days—and of your marriage? And what joys are you looking forward to in the days ahead?

❖   Think back on your experience with *Love and War*. What would you say are the highlights for you, the things God spoke to you through?

THE CORE IDEAS

- The secret to life is this—we are here in order to learn how to love. This is the great shift, the most fundamental realignment of our heart's ambitions.

- Love plays itself out in a thousand little choices, unseen and *without* supporting soundtrack. That's what makes it so beautiful.

(cont.)

- If there's to be an awakening of hope and desire, if there are to be some new frontiers in your relationship where you can talk about difficult things or you can handle conflict differently or approach sex differently, it is going to come through forgiveness.

- We are going to need a very compelling reason to lay down our lives, day after day, year after year. What could be more compelling than this? When we abandon ourselves to love, we find ourselves closer to the One who is always doing that himself. We find God.

- We live in a love story, set in the midst of war. Love is our destiny, and all hell it set against it.

GROUP TIME

Watch the session eight video together. If you would like, use the following space to take notes on anything that stood out to you.

After watching the video, discuss as a group any or all of the following questions:

1. Let's start with a first reaction. What spoke to you in this week's chapter, or this video session?

2. Given that this is our last official time together, let's start here: What has been the impact of this experience on you, and on your marriage?

3. In this session, the group talked about the thousand little choices they are making toward love. What jumped out at you?

4. Stasi said in the group how aware she is it is a thousand little choices in a day. Unseen *by* your spouse. But they are choices *for* your spouse. Can you relate?

5. Several weeks ago we talked about the things we do that drive each other crazy. Thinking about those things, what are some of the little choices you can make toward love?

6. In the chapter and in the questions you answered in the guide for this session, you gave some thought to forgiveness. While now is not the time to ask that forgiveness, let's talk about doing it soon. How do you feel about that? What will help that conversation go better?

7. The book ends with these words:

   We live in a love story, set in the midst of war. Love is our destiny, and all hell is set against it. Really, it explains so much. We wake each morning and find that we have to fight our way back to all that is true, fight off the thousand reasons to settle for less than the life we were created for. Our bodies awaken but then our hearts and souls must awaken, too, so that we might play our part in the Grand Affair. And God has made our hearts in such a way that nothing awakens us quite like some great mission which is ours alone to fulfill. Thus the power of fairy tales, all of which turn on this awakening in the heart on the boy and girl.

How is this shaping your perspective of life these days—and of your marriage?

8. And what joys are you looking forward to in the days ahead?

9. This is our last week together. Where would you like to go from here? Some options would be to take a break, then do another book study together. Or, the women could meet and do John and Stasi's book *Captivating* and the guys could meet and go through John's book *Wild at Heart.* What are your desires?

AFTERWARD

❖ What would you like to talk to your spouse about? Maybe the two of you could talk about the experience—what has God said and done through *Love and War?*

❖ It might be good to talk about your desires—what is it you are hoping for in your marriage?

There lingers yet the issue of forgiveness:

We need to bring the healing grace of forgiveness into our marriages. What that looks like is sitting down together and putting something on the table: "Honey, I think maybe this (you will need to be specific) has been doing damage and I'm only now realizing it." Or asking your mate, "What's it like to live with me? What has been the cumulative effective upon you?" And if you are fortunate enough for your spouse to take the enormous risk of telling you, DO NOT do further damage by explaining it away or defending yourself. "Well, now hang on a second—you've got your issues, too," or "That's not what I meant at all—you took that totally wrong!"

Listen to what they have to say, acknowledge the weight of it, and then say, "Sweetheart, I hear you. I am terribly sorry. Please, forgive me."

Timing is important. You want this to go well. When do you broach the subject? Talk to God about that. Pray beforehand. Pray hard.

And what *follows* is equally important. You don't want to sabotage the healing by repeating the very thing you did that caused you to ask for mercy in the first place. Your spouse needs to see real change; they need to see some conscious effort on your part or the Enemy will be there in a flash with all the old agreements: *You see? Things will never change. Forget it. It's not worth it.*

Calm down. Take a deep breath. We know this sounds like a root canal without Novocain, but God is with you. You are loved. You are forgiven. You are secure. You just have a little making up to do.

Maybe not driving home, but soon you may want to set time aside for this.

ACTIVITY:

What are you looking forward to in your marriage? The two of you need something out there, ahead of you that you are both dreaming about. Is it time for a second honeymoon? Maybe just a weekend away? Plan something you can both look forward to!

Where do we go from here?

Stasi and I, and the team at our ministry, have all sorts of resources for you—retreats for men and women; podcasts; online community; audio series; blogs; more videos and books—all sorts of great stuff! Come by and see us at www.ransomedheart.com!

NOTES

NOTES

NOTES

NOTES

NOTES

NOTES